NATIONAL GEOGRAPHIC

T0052334

Who Looks After Me?

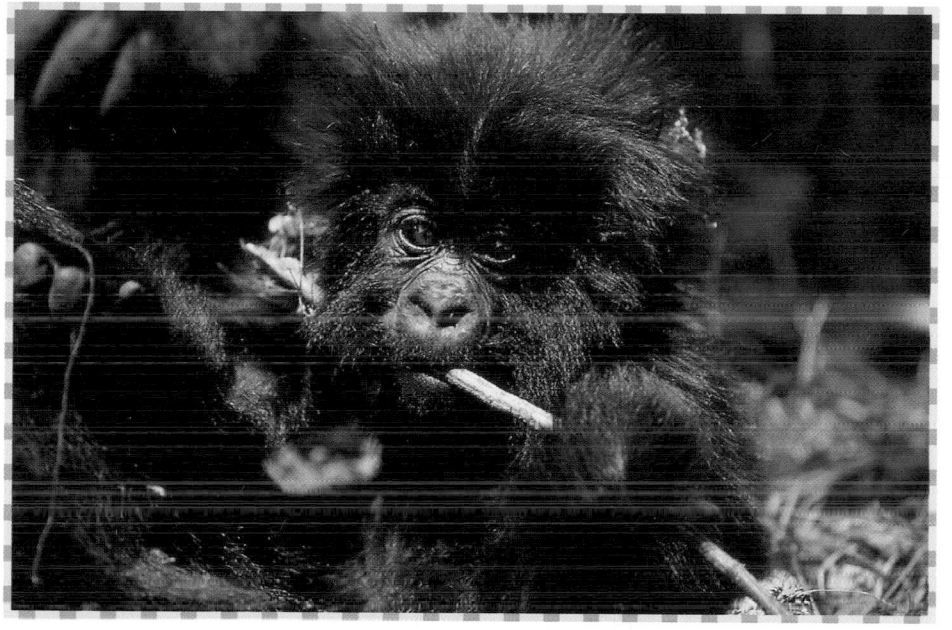

Dimi Stanos

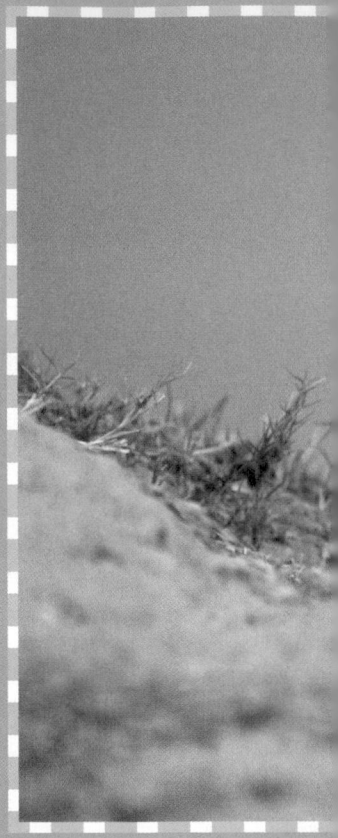

2

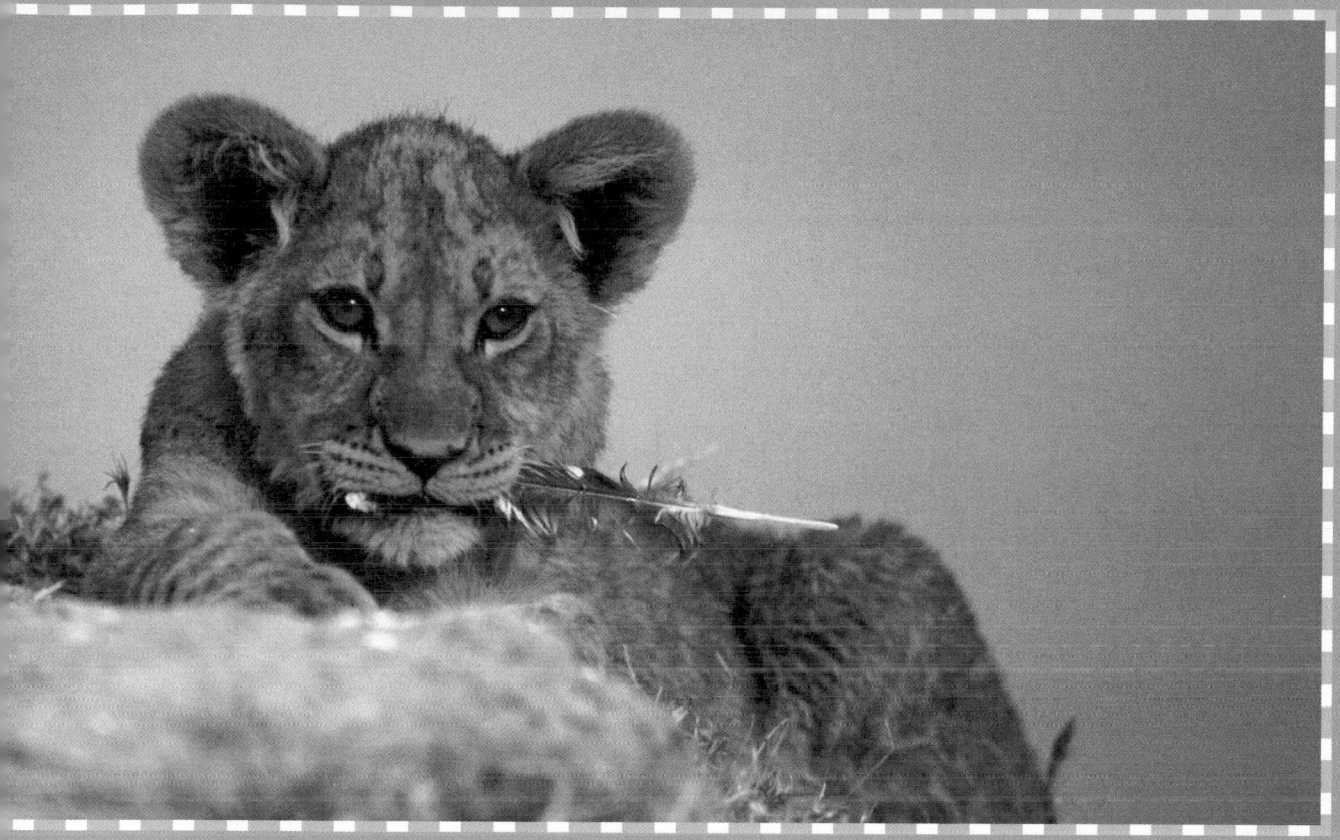

Who looks after me?

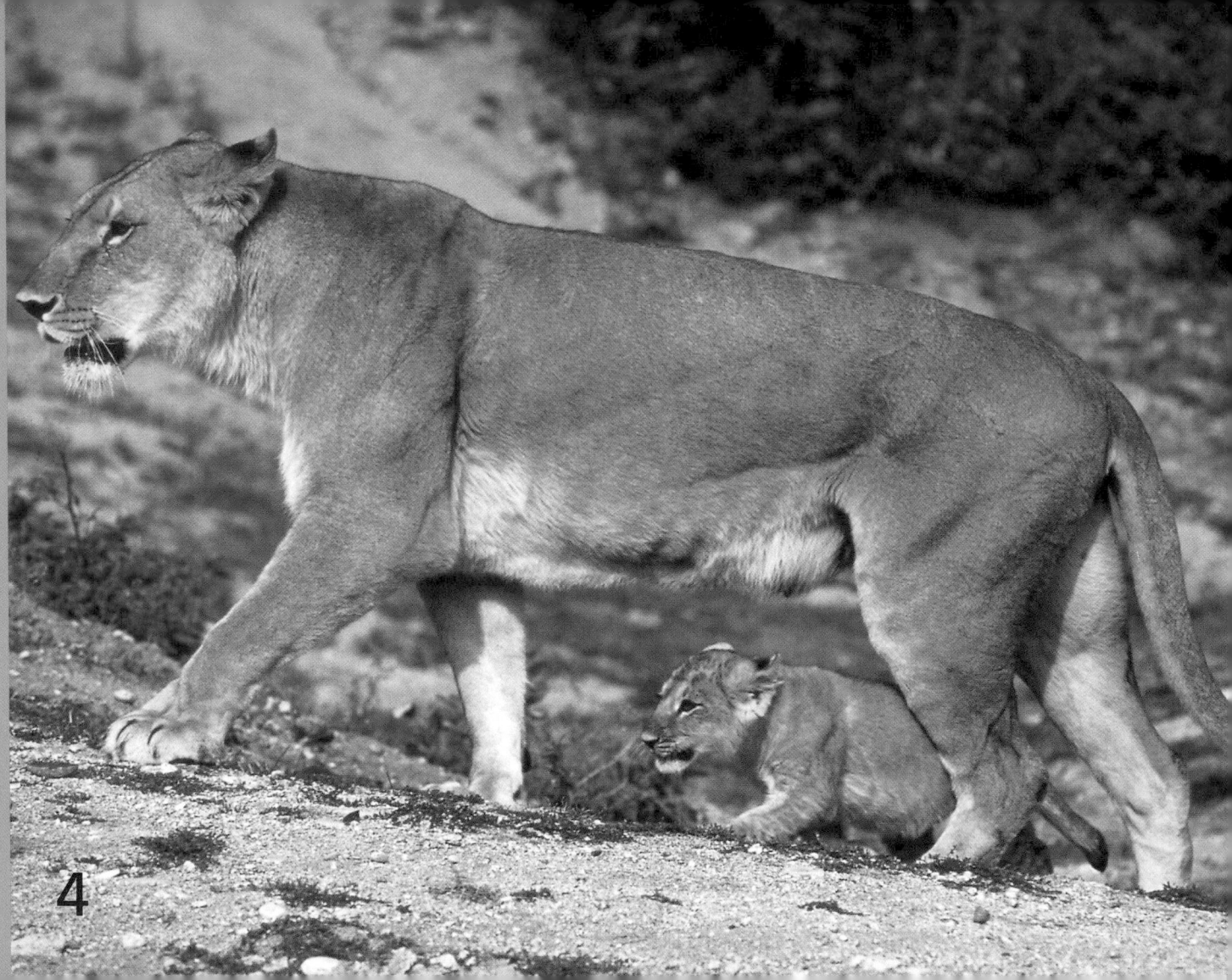

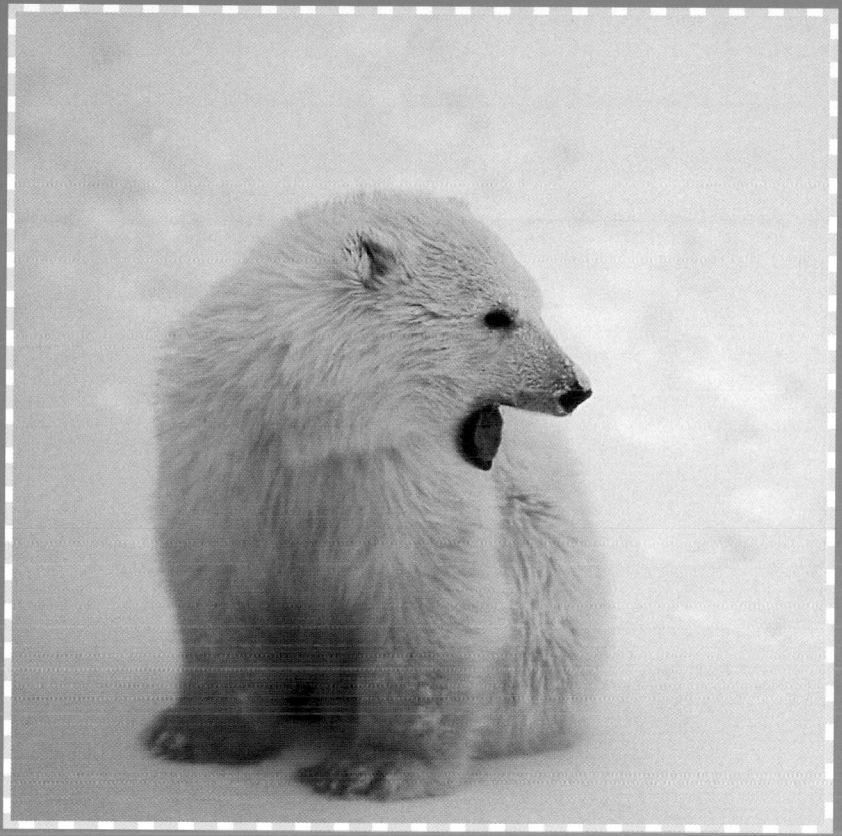

Who looks after me?

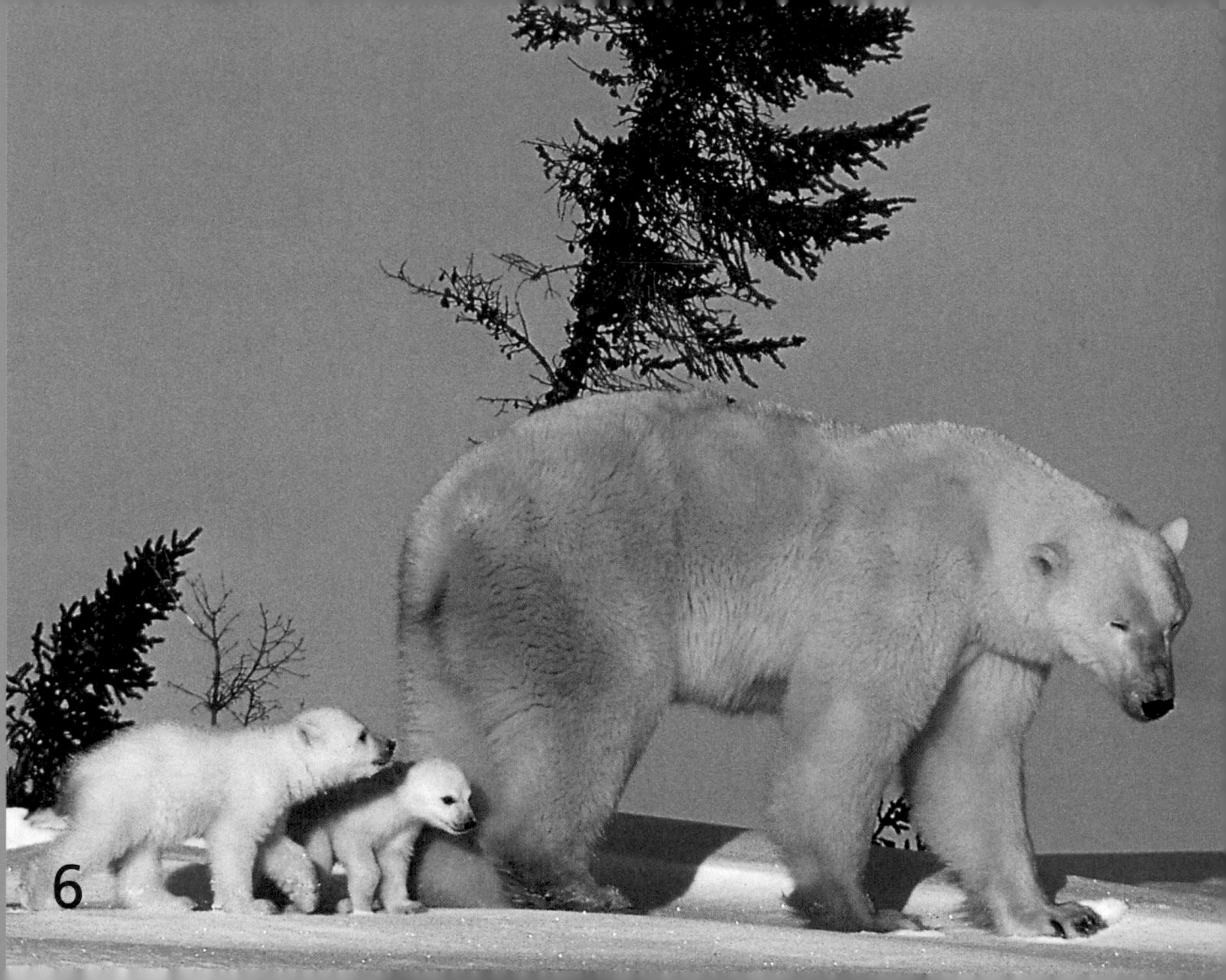

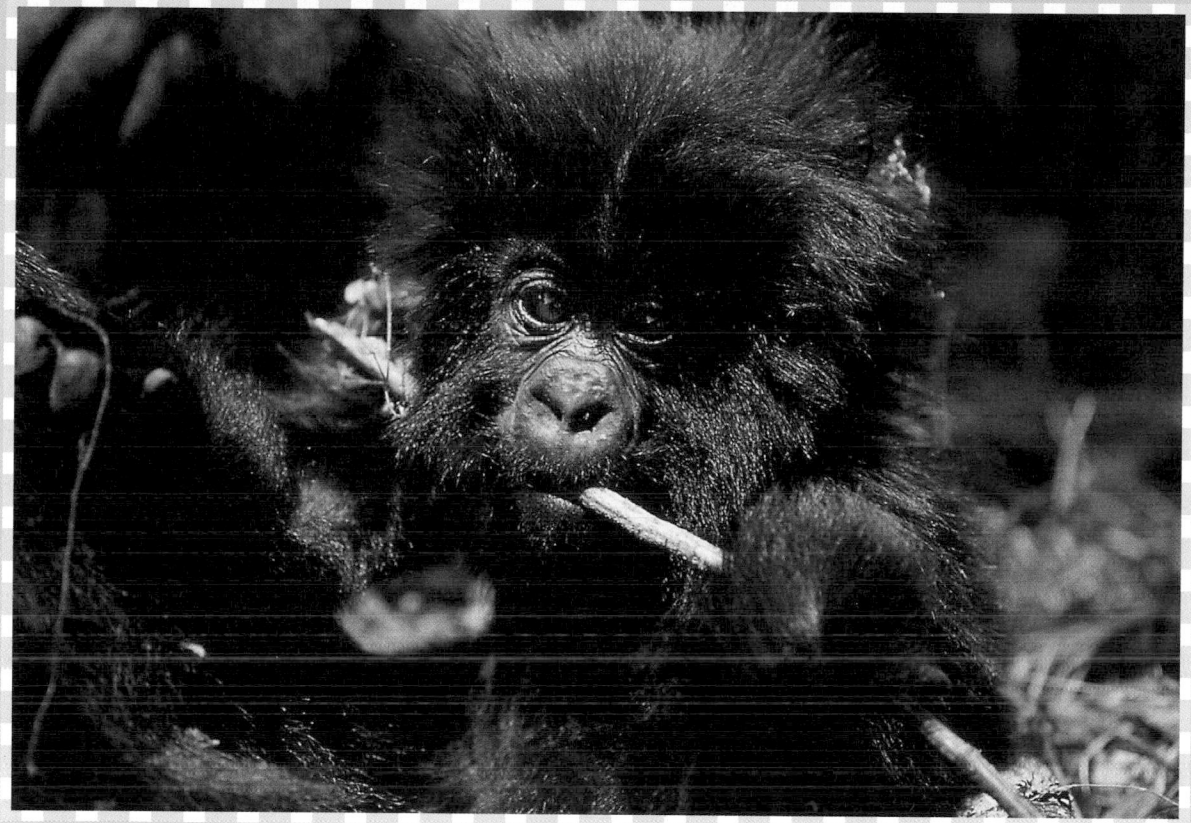

Who looks after me?

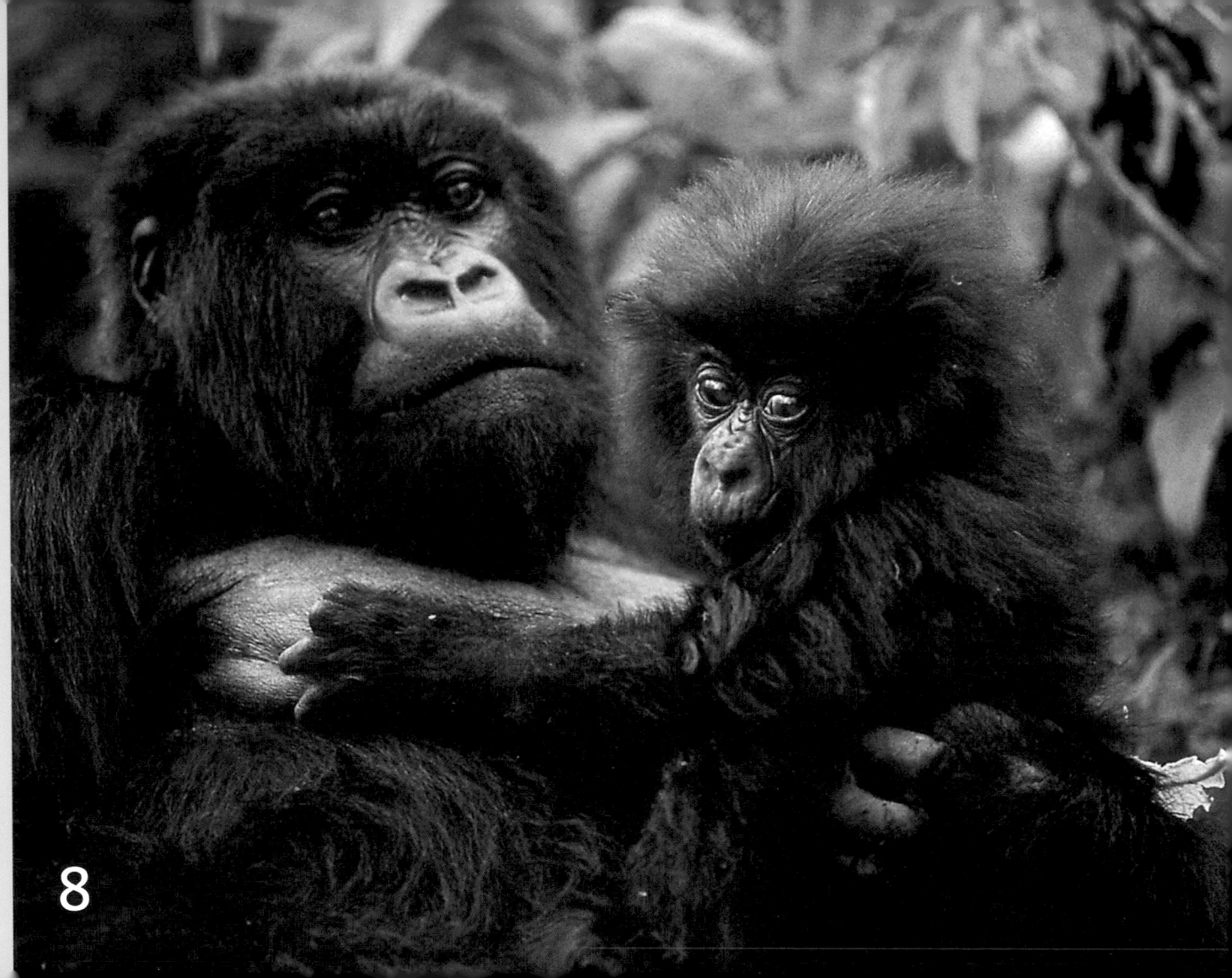

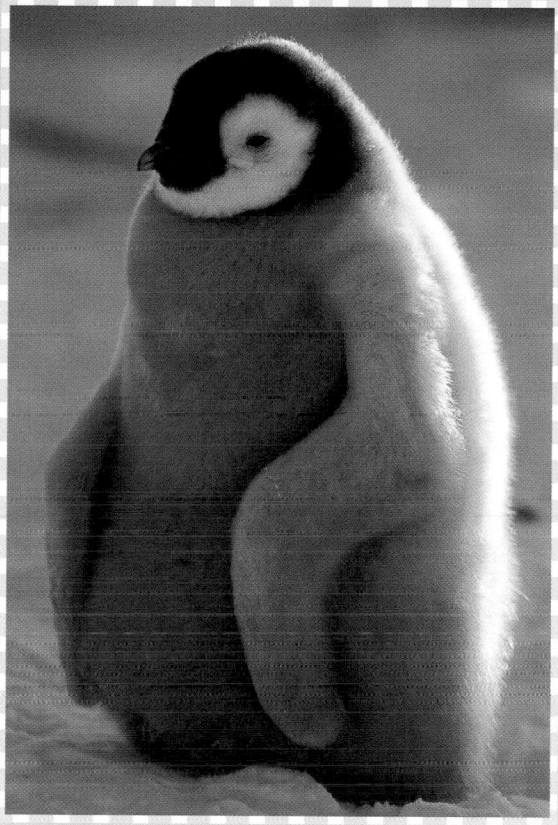

Who looks after me?

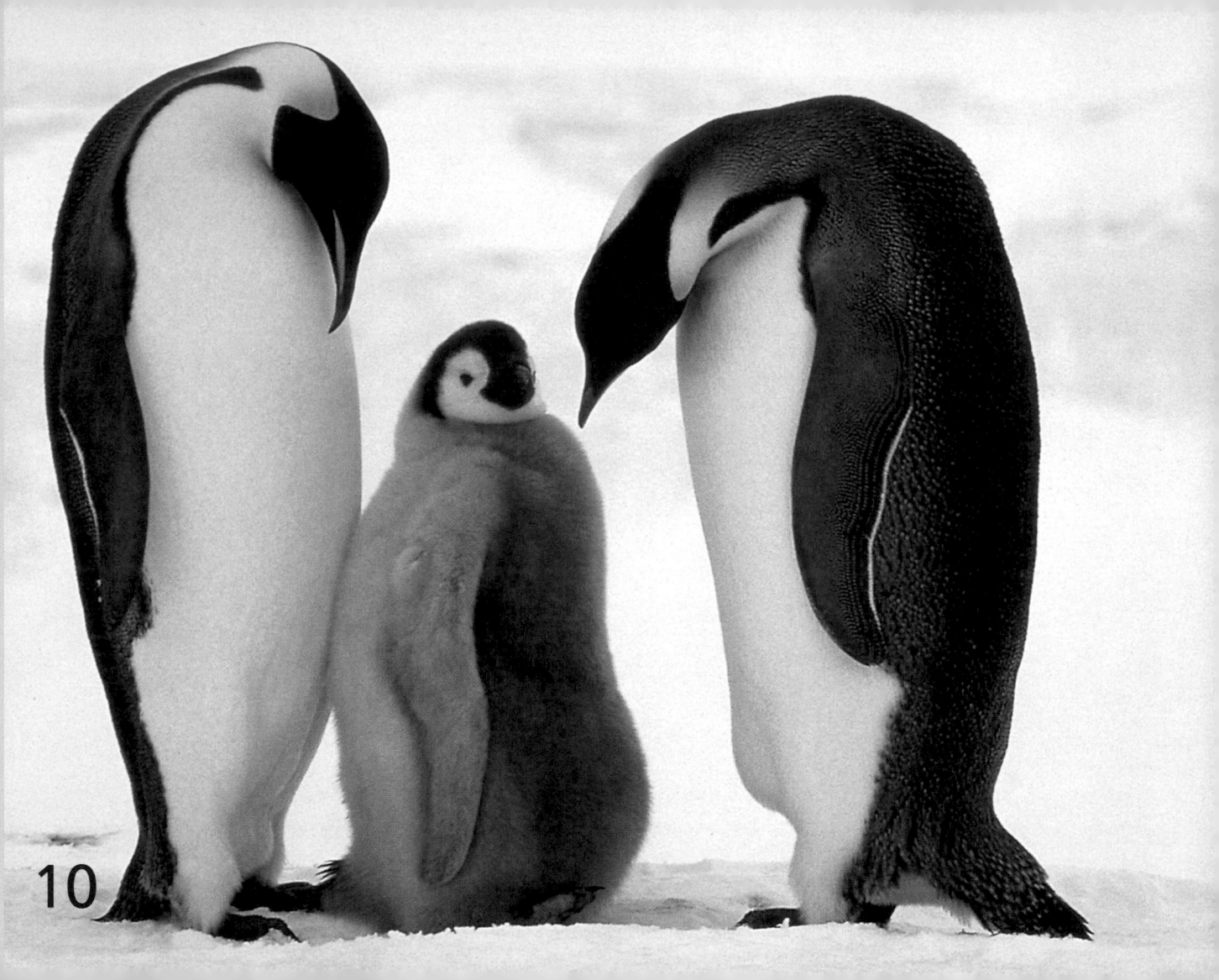

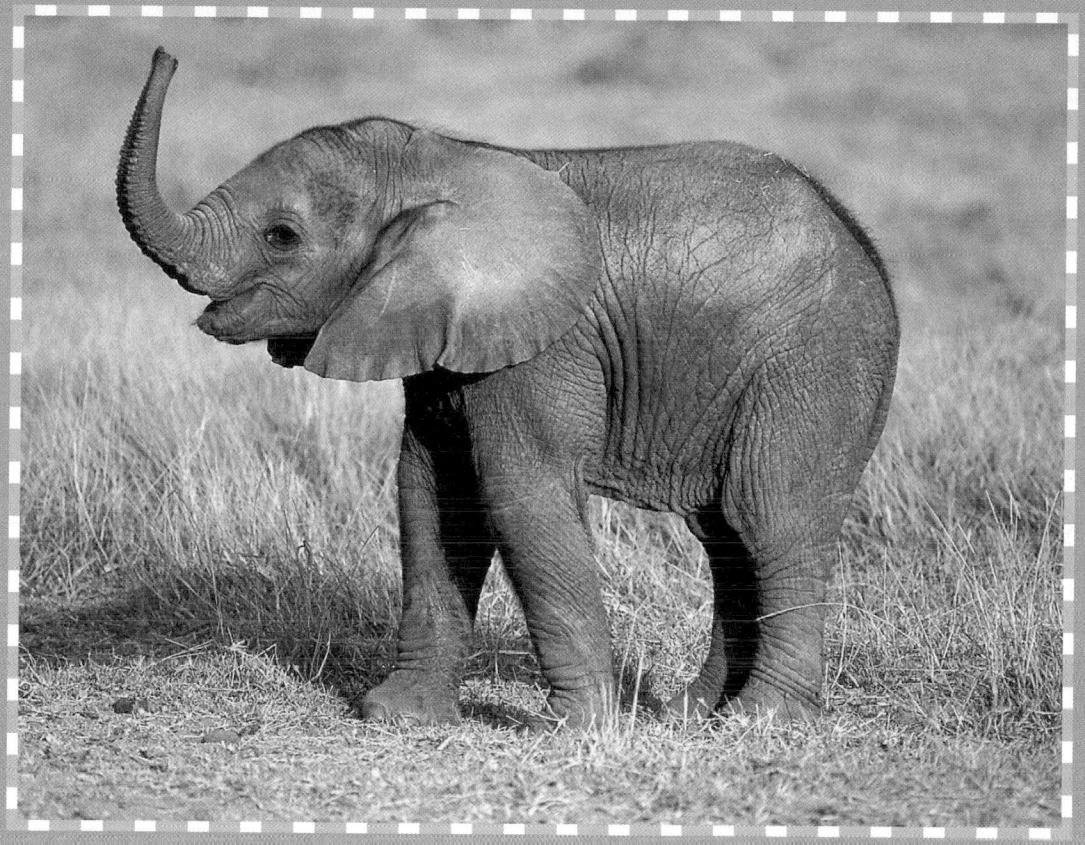

Who looks after me?

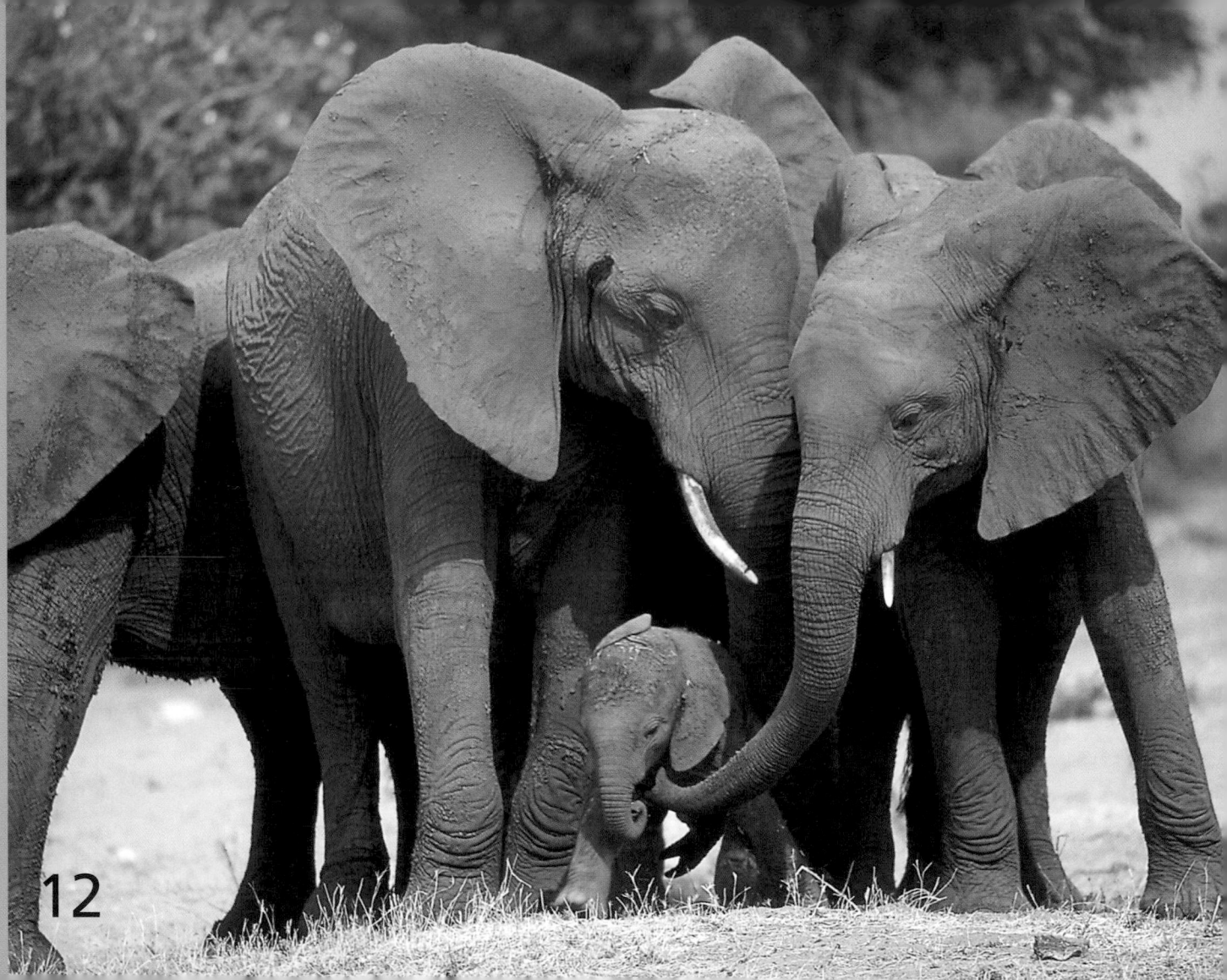